Swale

New Issues Poetry & Prose

Editor	Nancy Eimers
Managing Editor	Kimberly Kolbe
Assistant Editor	Abigail Goodhart
Layout Editor	Abigail Goodhart

New Issues Poetry & Prose
The College of Arts and Sciences
Western Michigan University
Kalamazoo, MI 49008

First Edition, 2020.

ISBN-13   978-1-936970-68-1 (paperbound)

Library of Congress Cataloging-in-Publication Data:
Hutchcraft, Allison
Swale/Allison Hutchcraft
Library of Congress Control Number: 2020938662

Art Director	Nick Kuder
Designer	Palou A. Craig
Production Manager	Paul Sizer
	The Design Center, Frostic School of Art
	College of Fine Arts
	Western Michigan University
Printing:	Books International

Swale

Allison Hutchcraft

New Issues Press

WESTERN MICHIGAN UNIVERSITY

for Juan

Contents

III

So Legged and Footed

Acknowledgments

Thank you to the editors of the journals in which the following poems first appeared, sometimes in earlier forms:

Barrow Street: "Flock or Herd, They Came to Me" and "From an Age of Sail"
Boulevard: "Calenture"
Cimarron Review: "Forest Rising from Its Name" and "When Living in Bear Country"
The Cincinnati Review: "As Knock-Kneed" and "As Twin Horses" (as "Self-Portrait as Knock-Kneed" and "Self-Portrait as Twin Horses")
Crazyhorse: "As Foxhound" and "As Lamb in Field" (as "Self-Portrait as Foxhound" and "Self-Portrait as Lamb and Ear")
Five Points: "So I Try to Picture the Priests"
The Gettysburg Review: "Alice among the Graves" (as "Among the Graves"), "The Lapis Lazuli in Which She Dreamed," and "The Mermaids at Weeki Wachee"
Image: "Reliquary"
Kenyon Review: "Dodo, *duodo,* sluggard," "Oh, Dodo. You can't," "Out the birds, out," "Seeds, or the collapsed bodies," "So legged, so footed, and who's left to care?," "Swampland. Bog. Mare aux Songes. 'Sea of dreams,'" and "You, again"
The Missouri Review: "Ghost Forest," "'I have written myself into a Tropical glow,'" "Scurvy," "Swale," and "You Like to Think the Whales Are Listening"
Poetry Northwest: "On This One Acre of the World"
The Southern Review: "Steller and the Sea Cow"
Third Coast: "Alice in Millefleurs"
Western Humanities Review: "Alice in the Cloisters"

"Calenture" was featured on *Verse Daily*, and "So legged, so footed, and who's left to care?" was featured on *Poetry Daily*.

For invaluable gifts of time, creative sanctuary, and financial support, I am grateful to the North Carolina Arts & Science Council, the Arts & Science Council for the City of Charlotte and Mecklenburg County, the Community of Writers, the Key West Literary Seminar, the Tin House Writers Workshop, the Hambidge Center for the Creative Arts & Sciences, and the Sitka Center for Art and Ecology. To my brilliant co-residents at Hambidge and Sitka: how lucky I am to have met you in amongst the trees.

Sincere appreciation and thanks to my friends and colleagues at the University of North Carolina at Charlotte, especially Chris Davis, and to my students.

Thank you to Nancy Eimers for belief in this manuscript and unparalleled kindness, and to the extraordinary team at New Issues, who bring books into the world. Thank you, Palou Craig, for your art.

Deepest gratitude to my teachers, whose generosity and vision continue to inspire and guide, especially Mary Szybist, Marianne Boruch, Donald Platt, Mary Leader, and Rishona Zimring.

Enormous thanks to the MFA program at Purdue University, and to the poets and writers whom I lived and learned alongside there. To my poetry group—Peter Blair, Beth Gargano, Pamela Richardson, and Gretchen Steele Pratt—and Amie Whittemore, who generously read so many of these poems and made them better.

Thank you, Amy, for wisdom and kindness. For loving friendship that sustains and has stretched far over the years, my endless thanks to Erin Glavich, Katie Perkins, Stasia Honnold, Ayla Terry-Mitchell, Miya Barnett, Kristin Griffin, and Lindsey Alexander, who has also read and encouraged more poems than I can count.

To Pepette, cat extraordinaire and third creature in our trio.

To my parents, Maureen and David Hutchcraft, and my sister, Christy, with love and admiration.

And to Juan, my companion in this life: thank you for the light you are and give, for great joy and laughter, compassion and love, and so much more.

Whirl up, sea—
whirl your pointed pines,
splash your great pines
on our rocks,
hurl your green over us,
cover us with your pools of fir.

—H. D.

Anchored here
in the rise and sink
    of life—

—Lorine Niedecker

Calenture

I shouldn't like to think of them, but I do—

the men who spent their days as sailors,
pacing the decks of their ships, who sometimes would get
a certain kind of sickness that made the sea
a field. How much
the mind wants land after so much stretch
of water, wants the most land-ish thing:

a field thick with witchgrass
or blonding wheat, a meadow silent
but for the ticking of insects.

It must have felt like bliss,
that first sight of the field so wide, like a yawn
that never closes.

Some say ships carried tufts of earth on board
to bathe those afflicted, or, when they finally reached shore,
pressed the sailors' faces down into the dirt.

From *calentura*, Spanish for fever.
Those affected had a fierce look.

I know I shouldn't like to think of those men—

but what it must have felt like—
the field green and
glinting in that sun,

the few seconds in the air
before they'd drop
into those reedy waves,

the unshorn grasses, their bare,
unsinkable sway.

Sometimes My Body Lifts as a Wave

and I name that wave Alice.
Summer of swine flu, summer of fear
coming down like a cloth—I watch

blue surgical masks cover mouths
in Arrivals, cover bundles of lost
minutes, fluorescent play of nerves.

Deplaning in Managua, we're ushered
in front of infrared cameras searching
for fever. Our heat blooms,

projected on a screen, red waves
radiating from armpits and chest,
appendages rimmed in green haloes.

That flare, lit from the inside—
how can it be I feel
Alice disappear?

Later, in Granada, where churches
used to burn, century-old smoke
still wisps the spires.

Another crazed American
William Walker set fire to the city
then staked a sign in what was

left of the square:
Aquí fue Granada.
Still, I eat

in a restaurant with tourists like me,
facing a wall where Walker was shot
at but not yet killed, the plaster

spackled with bullet holes. The flares
of what turns a city to flame disturb my sleep
but not enough.

In a church on Ometepe,
the island inside a lake
pulsing with volcanoes, my limbs

again lift, the walls
enormous, each rafter exposed.
At the front: life-sized wooden statues—

Mary without hands,
Jesus's head encircled
with a pink plastic bag.

So I Try to Picture the Priests

the way they might have been then—
in the Orinoco rainforest, tucked in dense

foliage and air thickened with bird calls.
The ramshackle priests in their dilapidated churches,

water-swollen wood, roofs falling in, and dusty
cleared-out courtyards for which they had razed

every tree, hanging from exposed beams and bare
balconies lamps lit with turtle oil, having plundered

nest upon nest for eggs. Perhaps the sand
the mothers' muscled flippers raked and dug

was damp, the tide lapping in, lick of foam
at the end of each wave.

Then hands quicker than scavenging
birds, than iguanas and sharks, whole schools

of fish unfurling, quick-changing in the current
like a silver curtain. It's possible

the moon was buried behind sifting clouds,
that howler monkeys loosened

their shrieks from the trees, dark-toed
sloths hanging on. But, for certain, there were

the priests—cracking open turtle shells,
separating rich fatty liquid from the embryos

inside, scooping out the slippery young, slime
under their fingernails

and dirt. Their hands keep filling. I don't
look away. Eggs, moons laid in sand.

On the New Continent, Our Eyes Shining

The animals we love most
we put in cages. Monkeys,
birds, bright salamanders.

The monkeys reach
through the meshed
reeds of their cages

for fruit hanging heavy
on trees we pass
beneath. Husks, seed

cases—butterfly wings
desiccate like bleached
pages. Bottles burst and

insects scatter. Monkeys
tumble out from cages
or fail to wake from sleep.

The air is thick, a humidity
curls all our dull
pages. Shadows dissipate

like dew and birds, bedeviled,
spring squawking from
our hands. The animals we

love we put in cages—
parrot, spoonbill, snake, all
on the backs of our porters.

Under fanned palms, among
herons, we find eels, heads
as thick as their tails. We are

told they are electric,
muscles flickering in mud.
We shove the horses in

to see, watch them leap
and writhe. The strong
ones survive. Our horses

don't fit in cages,
some trample and some
drown. What we

want we put in cages,
what we love desiccates
to bleached pages.

Scurvy

The tenderest sight argues ye clearest fantasie
of things visible. So Newton said, before or after sticking
pins into his eyes

for sake of science. I think I never loved
a thing that much:

not like the sailors plagued with scurvy
who died at the moment they reached
what they wanted most.

I try to think of them tender:

the sick man dreaming so long of the fruit,
its sunset edges and ripened pulse, rippled with seeds,
that he dies from the first slice
laid out on his tongue.

Likewise the wish for water—
water clear of salt, unstale and unbarreled,
water poured from porcelain to hand,
from hand to lips,
water that is sweet because
it is nothing—
that kills, too.

Often sailors lay deep in a reverie of home so real—
homestead, village, prairie,
land on which they once caught beetles creeping over mud,
hid stones in rough grasses—

only to wake to the ship's damp disaster,
the body a nesting of scars and bruises,
thighs chafed, groin blackened.

Who can blame a body
for what the mind can't undo?

No wonder it's then death took them—
first sight of land rising from the sea,
green and enameled, spilling over with trees.

"I have written myself into a Tropical glow"

—after Darwin

The sea is laced in phosphorescence
little galaxies afloat in the swell.
Insects click their invisible tongues
to wake the silken light—
volcano fire and lizard belly,
dusky skies softening, bats
unfolding, descending
as the barometer drops, stars pinned
to their velvety seats.

And the air scented, swallowed, insects falling
into the open mouths of waxy orchid
blossoms, spiny bromeliads, water pooling
into sticky pitcher plants, tendrils curling,
frogs bleating their mourning songs, the bleat
that rises, billowing, filling
the air like a flag, or swelling like a sail—

To not think of myself even for an hour—
but of fireflies lighting the understory
and everything tinged with this
tropical glow—haloed,
hallowed, steeped in birdsong,
the palm fronds pressing against the sky
as if this world were glass and breath
alone could make it flame.

Steller and the Sea Cow

To be thorough, a naturalist must sometimes kill,
piling up birds, toads, fire-striped salamanders, to procure
the best specimen. Shipwrecked,

Steller, too, was meticulous, climbing the carcass of the sea
cow, which they had dragged onto the beach
by a hook, their knives tearing the flesh less

when the cow at last stopped thrashing.

It was hard work, perhaps not worth
the tobacco he promised the men
for their labor. Afterwards, they returned

to their true task—months still left to reconstruct the ship—
and the naturalist to his: measuring the animal
from tip to tail before opening her side
to excavate the organs.

Finally, Steller was alone enough
to note the thick, ridged cutis and lice-like parasites
feasting in the folds.

                             It was a topography he could
cut into: Tawny, black, he thought, like the skin of a smoked ham,
the cuticle bristling with small raised cups
and, deeper, tiny perforated holes, like those of a thimble.
The kind of hide, when hung up to dry,
you could strip like bark from a tree.

Where to begin?
Snout, lips villous and rough as a hairbrush that would not
soften when boiled, the tongue
dumb at the mouth of the throat. Nothing proved
too large, small, or crude:

not the stomach, once stuffed with seaweed,
in which multiple men could lie, nor

ulna, radius, forked tail,
nipples wide with lactation,
the delicate urethra emptying.

And when he dissected the head, how carefully he sliced
skin from the eye to see
the sticky lachrymal sac, large enough to hold a chestnut.

It took every effort: mounting again and again the height
of the abdomen, plunging the knife deep
into recesses between bones, into subcutaneous fat.

When punctured, the plush mammary glands released
what was left of their milk, and Steller found
that it was sweet: yellow, the color of light
through sheer curtains
to which he woke as a boy.

Imagine Steller, flush with his work,
ignoring the stench of dead sailors, half-buried
in the sand and scavenged by foxes,

as he stares out to the sea,
to the rocky cliffs studded
with mammoth bones, to the sea cows still alive
and feeding,
the seals curling under the waves, the fog lifting
into what the future will be.

The Mermaids at Weeki Wachee

On distant ships, sailors once thought manatees
mermaids, the way they raised their heads
above the waves, as if beckoning,

their silhouettes stained with sunlight
and shadow.

The manatees buoyant, suspended as they fed
on shoal weed, water lettuce, musk and turtle grasses—
all the tender prairies of the sea.

                              Columbus in his journal thought
"but they are not so beautiful," remarking
"their faces had some masculine traits."

Still, the image settles like a slick of oil
on water, a light silica sheen, the sea

heavy with this iridescent skin.

                    *

But they are not so beautiful. Newt Perry knew this
when he opened his park at Weeki Wachee Springs
in the coastal hardwoods of segregated Florida, 1947

where land was cheap and clogged
with trash. He built his underwater theatre
into the spring's eye of light
and trained his mermaids to hold

their breath for minutes, gulping
air from submerged hoses
which they clutched like umbilical cords.

How they learned to perfect

strings of subaqueous tricks:
drinking bottles of Grapette and snacking
on bananas, turning their bodies like slow-moving

Ferris wheels, rubber flippers hinged
to their feet.

Perry gave them the usual props:

flashing mirrors and sequined tops,
giant open clam shells over which they hovered
like Venus in multiple,

                              a castle where they could swim
through every window.

In those early days, the mermaids ran
out to highway 19 to call in the cars,
the asphalt scalding their feet.

*

On another coast, I watch a livestream
on the "Save the Manatee" website and hope
one will swim into the frame.

The riverbed is a topography:
like a drowned moor, the sand, abstracted, a thin covering
of snow

                over which manatees appear
and dissolve, water grayed with haze
and sluiced by stripes of sun.

I think they must be hewn from moons—
their massive bodies floating
in this other sky, their backs marbled

with moss and white boat-inflicted scars:
a language by which scientists
tell them apart.

Haloes of blue gill huddle
around their weight, nibble
on algae, parasites, dead skin: a delicate slough

before the rounded tails, like giant rattan fans,
pulse out of view—

                    Unmanned,
the underwater camera cannot
swivel for the best shot—

until all that's left is the muffled spring,
and patches of light on the water

like sunken clouds
from airplane windows.

                    *

"Weeki Wachee," *little spring*
or *winding river*—

the name the Seminole gave this place

before those wars were waged, the terrible crush
to reservations, to land-locked
Oklahoma.
                    There's so much I don't know.

Not the black and white and Technicolor prints
snapped as training began, not the mermaids-to-be
who sat distracted on the wooden dock

in bandeau suits, their hair curled
to their shoulders, still pinned
and dry. Not even the ruffle

of Weeki Wachee waters in that long-ago
sunlight, or how the girls learned to smile
underwater,

        to show their teeth,
the mid-century still poised
to begin—

       *

To reach disgust, you have to go deeper
into history, find Victorian sketches

of mermaids fashioned from animal parts: head and face
of orangutan, upper body of baboon,
stitched to a king salmon's tail.

Lately, biologists stitch together fins
severed by fishing line
and battering boat propellers,

        tick off sightings
on coastal waters, threading migratory patterns
like seams about
to burst.

*

Once I crossed a muddy field to watch
turtles spawn on a beach—
                        the grasses soaked in pre-dusk light, a cow knee-deep
            at the edge of the scene,
and thought myself a spectacle.

Once I paid a man
to shuttle me from one tiny
island to the next, and when we reached the islet
covered in monkeys and leggy trees

he reached over the lip of the boat
to offer a piece of fruit
                        and the closest monkey
took it, my dutiful

clapping
filling up the lake.

                *

I was never like those girls, at home
in the water, so tan and long-haired and
glistening

but I learned to be alone
with aloneness, would wish every breeze take me under
its swell, the sky

scrubbed of clouds, the trees, admonished, when you caught
them breathing. Now I can't stop

thinking of what swallows
everything: the desire for the world
to be more than the world

and the spring, so clear and blameless, in which animals
drowned, the diver who emerged,
triumphant,

having pulled from the silty bottom
the whitened jaw of a mastodon.

*

Before the bluegills died off,
the eelgrass killed by algae blooms, the brown sludge
of development's runoff,

a mermaid could float,
held by the well
of water blooming—

those hills still alive and green
like grasslands swallowed by sea,
the spring a prayer of glittering—

*

When Weeki Wachee nearly closed, gone belly-up
as the crowds stopped coming,
it took a campaign to save them. Now

articles proclaim the endangered
mermaids have made a comeback,
are once again thriving:

newly minted and touching-up
waterproof makeup, securing bikini strings.
They no longer wear flippers

but have become the real thing:
hoisting iridescent Lycra tails over legs and torso,
"what every girl wants to be."

Summers offer weekend retreats: *Sirens of the Deep*
for women over thirty
where they sing

For if I were a Weeki Wachee mermaid
Everyone would be in love with me.

First breath lessons, then poses
while wielding that infamous tail, letting the current
take up your hair—

On Sundays, a closing ceremony and photo
shoot, certificates and glossy prints.

*

Florida's governor calls them *a resource,*
like ore, lumber, natural gas—

or groves of avocado trees, miles of pasture
on which cattle graze.

And it's true: the manatees
reel in tourists with their siren song,
call in droves for their chance to swim
with the giants they call gentle.

Sometimes it's better as a wish—

the audience rapt and waiting
for the show to begin, bound as if to masts
on the other side of glass

as the spring clears, its eddies and meadows,
for the bodies beneath—

I can hear the sea cows singing each to each—

We are underwater.
I am taught to breathe
and clap, smile, and wish

for another world. Can you feel how close
it might be? That someday, the promise
of everything.

II

The Trouble Is I

cannot turn off
what does not have a dial.
My mind goes

on, shameless and indiscreet, like TV
weather. I lounge
all day, make papier-mâché

animals that look out through web-
darkened windows.
Who will clean

the spiders out, unrustle
the leaves that have lodged there?
Nights, our new Southern

yard swells with too much
rain. The soil, clay-red
and dense, can't take any

more water in, is full
with flooding. When I rained
down hard, became pellets of flickering

hail, the earth did not
vanish but some slip
of me did. What

did you think of the orchids
when we saw them: a waxy-leafed sea inside
that greenhouse,

their paste-colored roots dividing
above our heads? Those roots looked dead
but how

can anything dead take all
the life
from the air?

Mornings, I forget to turn
to you but sometimes notice the way
the light grows like lichen

through the blinds.
Who thought we would live
differently? The pillow

makes a map of my face.

As Lamb in Field

Hot blade, hot lean
of metal—

shorn once,
and I gave myself

to shearing.
Were you the speckle

in our flock,
were you

the high, dry morning?
You rose

and sank, a kind
of sun

clearing daylight
from the dark.

Plump and dumb
in my wool,

in my curls,
I did not know

I was made from sky
till you

unclouded me
of fleece.

Soft-eared,
stuff-minded,

I was barely stirred
into my fatness

when you came,
through the grasses—

Alice in the Cloisters

One by one, shafts of sun shimmy up the walls,
and Alice counts the hours like a tongue

counts teeth. To fall asleep
in the lap of a paling sarcophagus, the body

stretched horizontal and nearly her height,
a stone dog lying loyal at her feet.

It's no surprise she wants to try on all
the pope's jackets resting quiet behind glass,

slip on enameled rings, shed her shoes and peer
straight into the sacristy. In the monastic gardens,

she loses her shadow amid the wattle of fences
and lady's bedstraw, each plot another diamond

of thinning lovage and shallot, milk thistle and rue.
Then all that cowslip, love-in-a-mist,

the poison plants of mandrake and deadly
nightshade, raised by invisible hands.

Isn't this the everything she nearly
wanted, mirage of the Hudson widening below

into white plain, the scanty light and birds
flitting through?

Here's her hour, her branch that could just
fit a dove—

Serfdom, fiefdom, barley and rye:
with Alice, everything eventually goes

out the window, through
the paint-cracked door.

Reliquary

Silver, shaped
    like a heart but now
empty, holding only some air,
    a lungful of sour breath

from someone who last breathed
    before the metal hinge
clicked shut. Or this, in the shape
    of a saint's forearm—

fashioned from gilded silver, niello,
    and gems, with a wood core—
how lifelike it looks: creased where the fingers
    fold, the half-moon of each

fingernail slightly raised…
    In procession, the lacquered
arm was raised high so that
    the crowds could see—

having waited in whirls of dust
    on the road, families straining
for a glimpse of what luck
    was promised to them.

Sometimes, small windows
    worked into the design—
miniature hinges and faux panes—
    opened

to show the bones inside:
        femur, forearm, shard
of clavicle and hip, knobs
        of knees and ankles,

rolling knucklebones:
        a piece
could make a township famous.
        But most precious

were the skulls, for which they
        also built likenesses,
hollowed busts elaborately
        painted, preserving lip

and eye color, the particular
        slope of a nose,
blond braids coiled like rope
        dipped in gold.

In Siena's basilica, Saint
        Catherine's head,
freed from its reliquary,
        now stands in its own

skin, incorrupt on the silver
        altar, the teeth still visible
in that open air. To get the head,
        the Sienese had to sever

it from the body and smuggle
        it out of Rome—
a *pious mutilation* ordained
        by the papacy.

Hatchet, saw, and blade
        sharpened for this work,
then the heft that leaned
        into the neck

to break the spinal cord.
        Catherine, patron
saint of safety
        from fire—

Once, smugglers
        hid the severed head
in a sack and, when the guards
        approached, prayed

for a miracle: their sack
        lightened, filled now
with rose petals—the color of
        a heart still burning.

As Knock-Kneed

I'm a foal—
they make my legs
move faster

by chiding them.
They wrap me up
from hoof to knee.

My longest memory—
long as the slick of black down my back—
was when the world slipped

out from over me.
Cold ground stunned.
Smells, now

sweetness,
mornings—
sugars and rum

on their fingers
and frost.
Still, their voices

beckon
Here, foal.
Down, foal.

When I break
they'll have a box for me.
When I falter—

pills and splints.
Here, foal—
Down, foal.

This is the way
a wind moves, in a box
and out of it.

Alice in Millefleurs

*—millefleurs, a "thousand flowers": a dense background of small
flowers and plants, frequently used in tapestries and other arts during
the Medieval Period*

Alice keeps close to the tapestry's border, the rabbits
in company balled-up like fists.

All the small, belly-full birds, dumb in their diminishment,
pile up like flotsam, and Alice hopes no one will notice

her here at the fabric's edge, solemn as a monk
and as eyeless. But no one is looking

for Alice. She knows not even starlings, all angle
and flight, will see her sweeping the bare spaces

between branches or unsettling the orange fruits that hang
like party ornaments, like glass bells without tongues

to ring them. She thinks: the air is stamped with birds
and trees. She thinks inside the seams, thousands

of flowers will continue to float uneasily in blue, as harts
and stags float, their pronged toes unable to find proper

ground. In the center, a man and a woman are trying
to bathe a falcon, but the bird is resisting, throwing

its wild wings up, all those silken feathers lifting
in peaks. The woman stirs the pool with a stick,

her companion holding the bird by legs wrapped
in red cord. Somewhere in Alice's thoughts,

where a wind begins to settle,
she remembers what she should not

remember: the sky this morning covered with blue-
black clouds, its lace of winter trees, and what

she heard of her mind, buzzing, as if
let out on a string.

Flock or Herd, They Came to Me

the horse in her cape and
the foal by her side, the fox
in black jacket and tails.

Each stood stiffly in starches, separate

as days, but the lambs
who laid back, trying
to become grass. How they all

held

out their wrists
to be
buttoned.

So I stitched for them suns

and on each sleeve
a moon
for when I met them.

Who, then, cast this shadow out?

It spread,
and stayed,
an illness settled

like sleep between us. I wanted

marriage, not
meanness, I wanted ribbons of luck
when they turned

down their heads to be petted.

But we grew bored
with our tea cups,
we grew bored with our beds.

We grew big

like wide water
reflecting
our moon-minds,

empty of thought.

The Lapis Lazuli in Which She Dreamed

Nun of the middle centuries,
    nameless scribe,
        who divided hours

into lines, parchment inked
    in script, serifs thin and nearly
        translucent

as insect wings. Moths to her
    candle, hoarfrost
        on warped monastery

windows. It's probably true she did not
    speak, at least in the silent
        scriptorium, where her

nimble fingers fashioned
    illuminated pages—
        saints and hooded

beasts, angels and men with their
    flattened faces, flattened
        feet, haloes of

hammered gold. She painted bones
    loosely in the skin, as if they too
        could fold,

tine over tine, like the delicate ribs of
    an accordion. It was she
        who worked

the lapis blue, grinding it to dust,
     pestle and bowl, dipping
          horsehair brush

into pigment, then sharpening the tip
     between her lips, her tongue
          and its secretions

leaving quick shards of ultramarine
     in the tartar
          of her teeth.

This is how we know
     she breathed—remains
          sifted from the sludge

of anonymous graves, gumless jaw-
     bone blooming under microscopes,
          unmasking residue

of precious stone. What's it like
     to be gone for good—
          name sandblasted

from the registry, brain for the last
     time hauled up
          from sleep?

On once-medieval plains: leaf
     rustle, nest of twigs, tilled
          soil—and, cloistered, farther

in, her bed, a pummeled sack
    of hay, where sometimes she felt
        flashes

of a god alight,
    soundless as a feather, hollow-
        spined.

Dead nun, those veils
    of paint, scraped skies,
        divine light:

the thoughts I think I could have had
    had I believed a blue
        celestial.

As Twin Horses

I have a bustle
round as a roast,

I have a fat stallion
combing my mane.

His teeth are white
and salty—his

horsefeet are breaking
open black keys.

I feel a radiation
on the breeze.

The lobster light
becomes us

and time retreats
like tundra.

The longer the stretch
the more I forget

that once we were two
horses

collecting the sun
on our sides.

Alice Goes for a Run, Considers the Year, How She Barely Shook

        free of herself
the whole time. Now die-hard moss that clings

   to up-branching trees, the bronzed chrysalis
        of another cicada sticking to a trunk,

        and flint-like gnats that float
like bits of ash through the air—

how she swallows them whole,
        calls each one her own: Alice,

        little Alice, taken down from their thrones.
It's been a year, and in that year, how everything felt

double-clung to itself, each movement forward
        shrunk to one more falling back,

        until Alice was a see-saw of herself
and nothing could ever be licked

or kicked clean. Mornings, she runs on Vail,
        on Colville, on curving Museum Drive

        because they have better trees, the real
Southern kind from what she's seen. Oaks, elms, creamy

magnolias: they are the only things bigger
        than the houses, each lined with invisible

fences, the begonias bright and neat.
Street by street, Alice notes the birdhouses

nailed directly into bark, then breath that burns
her throat to rust, all the buckled

sidewalk slabs, forced up
by roots—

On This One Acre of the World

To watch
   a woodpecker
      working on a tree—
to keep my eyes on its
   downward stripe,

the quick stutters
   of its head
      as it strikes over
and over the trunk—
   methodically

listening for insects
   inside, or the
      presence of sap,
a thickness that can be
   let out

with boring incisions,
   little holes
      the tree repairs
by a kind
   of bleeding.

To watch,
   but the mind
      moves on
so easily—
   to doubt rising

like a wave from the sea,
　　to the look you gave
　　　　when I knew
how much
　　I hurt you.

It has something to do
　　with perspective—
　　　　the palpable
world
　　getting smaller,

so small I forget
　　that downhill
　　　　in a house that is
dove-gray and spotted
　　with tree shadow,

someone is shaking
　　a sheet from a window—
　　　　see how the cotton rises
and snaps, hooks
　　onto the air.

Laundered, dried,
　　shaken—
　　　　how new
we might be,
　　how easily repaired.

Forest Rising from Its Name

And what if it weren't *pine*, nothing left
      to be pined for, no needles strewn about

like so many long-necked matchsticks, no cities
      inside fallen cones with a secret of sap.

What if the late seasons weren't grieved
      as ochre into brown, weren't old

photographs that keep fading, the summers I knew
      drying up like sandy creek beds.

To name nothing as lupine or paintbrush folded in
      the high grasses, no bees

searching for nectar, nor nuthatches, woodpeckers,
      crowned chickadees disappearing

into holes in these trees. If it weren't my mind
      moving like this wet slide, this

pool filling with snowmelt and algae covering
      stones, would there still be water

striders as I go under, their spindly legs
      casting their nets—

What if only lung, cavity, and chest—
      and alpine aster as it settles

into purple shadow, day gradually darkening,
    the wet body now cool

in the shade, each hair lifting
    as wind hits the skin.

When Living in Bear Country

you have to flick your spit
up in an arc, to make everything wide
and holy. It's like having a hinge in your side—

a little wasp or beetle that unwinds
or tightens with a key. Place the key in your breast
pocket, in amongst the bits of heather and clicking
rocks you stole from the river. Know that here
there are bears, of black fur and blond,
of rusty cinnamon,

and that they are hungry and don't need
you or what you want them to be. All day they forage
for anything with scent: dark juice of berries
or geometric caves of the comb, insects mid-flutter,
roots, pale from the ground...

As the forest cools into dusk, as brushy
hillsides quiet and long-legged deer
lie down at last, look for signs:

scat like a dog's, dismantled stumps,
boulders rolled over, hair clung
to trunks in a rough, shaggy gauze.

Close your eyes: you are never alone—
even the scavenging crows can't help
being alive.

Alice above Timberline

at last taller than the trees. This high up,
not much can grow—

not the puffed-out needles of Jeffrey pines
or the towering

ponderosas whose shadows she hiked
through, the sun at a slant.

All up the sandy trail, Alice took her time,
brushing past mule ears, their yellow

petals flagrant in summer, then whole boulders
spotted with lichen, bursts

of rusted orange like drops of paint pressed
down by a thumb.

Now, the hearty wild flowers that need no shade
huddle close to the ground,

now the twisted silver junipers are wind-wrung
as when someone wrenches

water from a cloth.
Everywhere, granite

slabs underfoot, but Alice keeps slipping, is
beginning to drift—

If only the ski town
could be held by a squint,

if only the compass dial would settle, not wobble
and spin.

How long until oxygen goes
thin, when breath

begins to catch—the tufts of trees still fanning
out below, each like a little

green explosion, or like nothing
at all.

As Foxhound

Bend. Bend. Bend. Barb—
Fox, what

made you disappear?
What snuck you from our mark?

You always go down to earth.
You always are burrowed and brooding.

Didn't they tell you—
you must be loose, for pursuit.

                          Bend bugles, burn brassy,
bend riders to silken my ears—

I have to snuff you out,
I have to think you

red
in the rough-tree thicket.

When Living in Bear Country

Though you don't even know it, though you don't like to pretend,
it's possible you wish a bear could break something right
out of you, as it does honey from a struck-open hive,
as it does the soft, dusty bodies of moths
swallowed whole. If you are quiet and not altogether used
to having your deepest grief eaten
and loved, try to imagine you can turn your head
towards that animal shoulder, can, even now, turn away
from what's yours.

III

Swale

In my winter by the sea, I fashioned
a new habit:

each day, walking to Crowley Creek through mud
and leafless alder, their branches

cupped by the plush green of mosses and rolling
beds of sword fern, whose serrated

edges thrust extravagantly into cold and humid air.
The creek fed the estuary,

which in turn fed the sea—and I liked to see how far up
the tide had reached,

or how far it had receded, the marshy banks transformed
by that lunar clockwork

on which my hours turned.
Water called *slack*, like the grip on a rope

loosened, at which point the river would swell
and still, the brackish tide

having expanded the limits of the creek, submerged
grasses swaying like the drowned

hair of a doll. Cold and hard and clear,
the water looked like the creek I felt in me.

Day after day I watched gulls float like wooden toys,
rocking on the unsteady surface,

and studied barnacles clasped to rocks, the
shell-white skeletons

of small shoreline animals, discarded limbs
of driftwood.

Swale also meaning a *depression*, a *low place*
in the land,

the sour smell once the water has drawn back,
unmasking river sludge

and battered sea debris:
luminous blue Velella

with their fan-like sails, hollow carapaces of crabs,
picked at and cleaned—

When I swale, I cannot
tell border from border, land

from water. I feel the loam
of day

crumble. Washed up, what's left?
An accumulation of silt. Or sand, sifted,

rubbery tendrils of seaweed dotted with notches
like taste buds inflamed—

Sometimes I think love is swale, and
sometimes sadness, how each

comes in like a tide, how each
alters the bodies beneath.

Heart, be complete, come out of your grave-light—
It was decades before I was alive

when the estuary was diked to make more
land for pasture, the water

no longer water then but fields of sown grasses
for the cows to eat. How they, too,

must have tasted it—the memory of water
buried in the new green shoots,

the verdant nourishment, still tasting, faintly,
of brine.

Ghost Forest

As if resurrected, the trees
    have returned: what's left
of their once buried trunks now
    jagging through beach sand.

We go at low tide so we
    can see them,
and it is easy to walk to those farthest
    up shore, to peer

into their hollows made by wind
    and by water, following
the ancient rings, the swollen
    wood, dark and soft,

something to flake with a tool
    or fingernail.
In all the available spaces,
    blue-gray stones,

the surprising white
    of shattered shells,
as if someone had lodged
    them there deliberately.

Delicate, bone-like, barnacles
    encase trunk after trunk,
each exoskeleton as small as a stud
    earring and open at the top,

like an erupted volcano or
        extracted molar.
Farther north, in the outskirts
        of Alaska's archipelagos,

if the earth ruptures
        we will feel it. The sea
will swell with tsunami waves,
        covering roads and towns,

breaking apart the shore
        as two thousand years ago
these spruce broke
        from high cliff shelves.

And when they were buried it was
        instantly—
flanks of land collapsing, swallowed,
        and the animals, too,

their pelty sinking.
        Called *ghost*, but look
how what's left stubbornly remains,
        not ghost at all but

solid, stunted branches, radial
        and smooth,
the polished wood now green
        with a fine algae

or limp strands of seaweed,
            which, when the tide returns, will rise
like candles taking flame.
            Look closer:

there is always something ready
            to bury us.
Slabs of damp sand break off
            into the creek

that cuts this beach in two—
            in the arctic, whole glaciers
fracture this way, the oceans
            everywhere rising.

A woman wades across
            the silty creek, carrying
her small dog in the cleft
            of her jacket—

her legs more and more
            submerged
nearly up to her hips now—
            the look on her face—

From an Age of Sail

I married my last anchor at breakfast, took
the car out, hung wash on the line. Still, I can't

un-glove this feeling or turn yeast into bread.
Do you also worry we'll become rueful,

improbable, unkind? Wild or not,
the future is always peopled with families.

Effusive and out of luck, their emanations
are Sundays on the eastern shore,

rolled-out towels and plastic coolers,
bodies stippling the sand like fleshy parking

cones. Come, let's weave our way among them
before the hour gets long and we start feeling

out of season. See how the skywriter trails off
from his own cloud? Words angle and stretch

but the beach-proud children don't even look
up, or know their goose-flesh skin is cold

in this wind. Meanwhile, stiff shrubbery
embroiders the dunes. I think I've had enough

of maritime days, of following constellations
like a map, of leaning hard into the wave.

I'd rather be taken apart like a watch,
my twelve shining parts laid out on a cloth.

Buoyed. Bankrupt. Out to sea.
When we finally come to,

all the mothers and fathers will be washing
our last spoons, emptying our drawers

of cotton underwear onto an unswept floor.
Our shirts left out to dry will be sheer

from weeks of heat shining through.
Our wide decks will be scrubbed

clean, our hands,
holding fast to invisible lines.

Polaris

The waves curl up
    then flatten back to blue.
        I count asteroids and sea

stars out loud, watch my breaths
    huddle into fog.
        The North Star blinks on

but is it true
    I've lost my way?
        Failed letters home,

a drooping sail,
    tangles in the rigging.
        I wonder what all

the mothers do
    with the regrets that they
        are mothers—

if they keep them somewhere safe
    and barely used
        like jewelry too fine

to wear—necklaces, pearls.
    See how they become more
        beautiful

and useless with time.
    When I think
        of what I ought to have

said or done but did not, or wouldn't,
    my worry becomes amber-like,
        smooth—

drop of hardened light
    I polish
        till it glows.

On Effort

What leans in and calls me by name as if I had a spirit
and not this wayward body

                    is also bruiseable, obedient, and
tired. To be self-satisfied, to be both the willow
and the arc of branches. What do I

believe in still?

               I once gave each leaf a different name
and numbered all the tulip bulbs. I sent the hunters away.

But now: shudder of sea grass. Pitches of widening dunes. I look
at the ocean and only see ocean. Edge that draws
closer, a blankness ensues.

                 And you, whom once I'd save,
whom I'd pluck out from the curling waves—

Strong swimmer, whoever thought you'd drown,
whoever thought you'd strain
for shore—

You Like to Think the Whales Are Listening

secure in their
        great weight. Consider
        the form,
the broad unflankable
        sides. Consider the way

the whale's body
        carries no worry
            of your world
over its thick purple skin,
        the blubber some vast

impenetrable stuffing
        between your heart
            and a heart you can't
see. You like to think
        of the teeth—

white and neat in that cold,
        where you can forget
            your own set of bones,
fingers and feet, and reach
        for something larger,

petal shape of fin,
        expanding fan of tail.
            It's possible to let go
of oxygen, too,
        at least the way you need it,

at least the way you gasp
    mid-sleep in the night
       as if you could
be like them, coming
    up for air—

You wouldn't know
    what to do,
       would you,
with all that quiet,
    that deep forgetting

of yourself,
    nestled, barely there—
       as if you were
another thorny appendage
    on the waves,

       a ship making way.

Ghost Lobster

To land one is good luck,
lobstermen say, a glowing oddity
pulled up from the sea

not in nets, but cages, chipped
metal hinges snagging with seaweed
then stacked on salty docks.

To catch lobsters is *to harvest,*
as it is to pluck pearls
from the soft bodies of oysters,

but when I try to imagine the ocean
being culled like fields of wheat for its crops—
those drowned cages sifting currents for what the sea might yield—
I come up empty.

It's easier to think
of the ghost lobsters, elusive, their white
translucent bodies, paling as any old t-shirt: something
to keep, like a shell picked up on a shoreline,
or a coin.

Lobstermen call them *ghosts,*
whites, crystals, harboring
the hope that one day they might
get one. Their days suddenly graced.

I could use a harbinger
of luck,
could net one now—

skirting the traps and scavenging monkfish,
just riding
the cool undercurrents of the mid-Atlantic, a glow
against the ocean floor,
which from here almost looks blue.

Dream from the Shade

Large birds with feathers of slick
oily blue veering into black,
their long bills and longer
necks, eyes watchful and clear.

Then their bodies' fluid motion—
duck and plunge and quick
ricochet—was a kind of dance,
playing with us
or warding us off—
I didn't know which.

In the pond or pool
tall dense weeds grew
up from the clay bottom, and when we jumped
in, they poked our legs and arms,
our feet.

Even the sun was a different color,
more buttery and clean,
and the way it glinted off the water
was what longing looks like
when found.

It's the kind you can never
go back to:

cool palm of water,
insistent sun,
the scratchy, verdant reeds
still growing.

A Color of Sunset

When I saw for myself
        it was spring.
The sun strangely warm
        that far north, heating

black rocks on the bank,
        the water cold and waving
as an excess of sea flowed
        back into the estuary.

First, a sudden splashing,
        then tangle
of slick otter bodies thrusting
        in the shallows.

It was hard to tell
        there were two,
to distinguish
        the flashing forms—

I thought *playing,*
        then *fighting:*
the funnel of fur
        increasingly rough.

But it was clear when one
        pulled the other
onto a half-submerged rock—
        twice as large

as the one to which it was
        fastened, heaved
over its back, holding
        the smaller body down.

I thought she would drown
        when they fell back
under, her cry
        continuous except

when muffled by water.
        I watched the tumult,
followed it down the current,
        the smaller body twice

dragged onto the bank. It took much more
        than minutes—
I had thought nature
        made it quick.

The cry like a drowning—I swear
        it drew a gurgle.
The red pink cavern
        of her mouth

glinting. When stillness
        finally came, there
was nothing left to see—
        only an otter's head

swimming away, dragging
    a ripple like an
elongated *V.* And soft wind through
    leafing alder, the cold

tide lapping. The round, exhausted
    stones, the color
of the sun setting, like a mouth
    pried open.

Sometimes I Am Permitted to Return to the Sea

Sometimes I am permitted to return to the sea
as if it were the bank of the world that
beckoned, as if I could ride its blue

as one climbs wind-shorn grasses, made
precipice, made headland crop, where ospreys
divide fields of sky, swooping then gliding

then absolutely still, as if held by strings,
a child's aeroplane treading air before it
dives, runnels and waves, white flicks flecking

the horizon line. The sea, where I am
no voice, am voiceless, buried by the sound
of water into wind, of earth and orbit sliding,

clumps of foam tossed over wet pitted
beach, flurry of sand crabs as the quick
water recedes. To return to this green

ledge falling from air, to turquoise and
cobalt sea, edge of every vanishing, cliffs
latticed with pines above the black

rocky cove, where waves break in fringes
of lace, where sunlight deepens furrows,
this flame, this sweep and slip of tidal sea.

Whale Fall

I'd like to think of our bones lit up from the inside,
calcium-rich, garden of fused coral.

Some mummies, I've learned, are preserved by mud,
their bodies suspended in the sleep
of a peat bog, while others lie harbored
in beds of ice or salt.

It's the skin that makes them so human, still there—
thick cap over jaw and forehead, the place where a nose jutted
before spongy cartilage slipped down
as sand erodes from a hill.

How difficult it is to see
the body unworn,
the last ribbon pulled through the air.
Maybe I'm not so much for the flesh—

When a whale carcass drops
to the ocean floor it's called *whale fall*
and seasons pass before the bones begin to show,
before those alien-white forms work through
like blisters of light.

Alice among the Graves

—Key West, Florida

The headstones, they crumble, they buckle
and lean. It must be

how things breathe here,
each mouthful of salt.

The cemetery tries
its best to be serene

with its benches and historic
plaques, the palm trees that rise

on thin, unknotted spines.
All those squat iron gates

hemming in the family plots—
they can't keep anything out,

not the lizards or birds, not
the brazen carpet of weeds.

Much worse than storms
are the gut-heavy

iguanas
crashing down from trees.

They like to nest under
the graves, heaving

accordion-like legs,
meaty and strange,

to scuttle between
the concrete blocks

and lay small seas
of eggs in the crumbs.

Half a mile away on White
Street, Civil

War soldiers killed
by yellow fever lie

unmarked in a yard,
a bevy of roosters crowing

above them in the grass,
kicking up dirt and leaves. What

the dead wouldn't
give for something promised:

starboard
or boat-sink,

the bleached tide
streaming in—

SO LEGGED AND FOOTED

Oh, Dodo. You can't

do what others do.
　　You're caught up
in a wild
　　bulb of a beak—

there are sunsets tied
　　to your
　　　　dum-dum feet.
Your dreams
　　are floral-scented.

Little wings, token
　　and tucked,
　　　　have they ever had
such fears of flying?
　　Why, this world

is strange—it tries me.
　　Dodo,
　　　　I miss you.
No one has your charm.
　　When I fell in love,

the earth was an iron-
　　blue bruise.
　　　　I can say this
to you, who expect nothing,
　　no new news.

Yes, it's better here
    on the ground.
        I was angled,
sun-stunned and tossed
    when I thought

I saw you
    sea-battered
        and streaming.
Your island was near
    and those oceans.

In my dreaming,
    you kept charging,
        then falling
asleep—
    blue-eyed and blunted.

Dodo, *duodo*, sluggard.

Fat-arse. Knot-bum. Fool.

But if *dodo, dodar, dodé* is

to falter, then I'm fowl-

feathered, grief-spent, spurned.

Who wouldn't think the world concave
and bluish? The sky a wave up from the sea
drawn back again. Thick salted air.

You carried your plumage like I carry
my sleeves—gray, ill-fitting at the seams.
Still, they called you *ostrich, rail,*

albatross, and *hen,* cursed your tough breast
meat, the wrinkle in your wings. Do you
remember the time one chased

you to their circle—sailor revelry and
smell—and held you up by one stubby leg
to dangle in the air? Island-crier, gray-coat,

how you sang out as you were lifted,
how all your kin, dispersed,
came running to you—

Swampland. Bog. Mare aux Songes. "Sea of dreams"

but the translation slips. I think *a song to sing*

before the singing's done, a mouth rounded out

like a coin. The history books all say the same

thing: first there was the *mare* then a man

who went wild in it, found it was a shallow

pool of bones, whole birds submerged, black

beaks & flightless wings. How he tried to gather

them up like wheat in his arms, like a woman

with sheets. Can I catalog what is not mine

to count. Can an island slide off in my sleep.

To dig more bones. That's what the men

were hired for. They found them with their feet.

Out into the swale of that swamp, stepping waist-

deep, water like a seam. Then all the battered

hollow limbs, the caved-in skulls, lifted

toward the light. What lets me dream

when the world keeps rolling out like a map

at both ends, this side curling, that side, warped.

Dodo, I do not doubt the earth,

but there is this continental slip.

I keep losing the headlands in the crook

of your beak, the coast lines get covered up

in your feathery scruff. Those men whose names

I cannot find. Were there two. Were there ten.

Who's to say from what, or when.

Out the birds, out

the stones. Out all
    things that can fly
        or be thrown.
But you—your woody-throat,
    your knotted toes.

Did you know
    where to go?
        Did your world
swing high,
    then low?

How the sky grew
    thick
        with people.
Everywhere a hand,
    a half-filled sail.

Now the hogs keep hogging
    all the fruit.
        The rats swing
like bats from the trees,
    the monkeys

eating everything green.
    Do you wish
        instead
you were a flying
    fish—a form that fills

sea-air
    with flashing
        gills? Or heavy
like trout, the ill-fitted
    eel? All day they gleam

in antique streams.
    Dodo,
        you are no cockatoo,
no home-bound
    hen. Your feathers

don't fluff enough—
    there's a troubling
        sheen
where your beak
    clamps shut.

For years: a coco-tree,
    a rotted branch,
        a lyre of weeds.
Then those pigs—
    voracious,

flattening the grass,
    sending their snouts
        into daybreak,
your home, uncovered,
    nested.

Seeds, or the collapsed bodies

of rotting fruit,

unearthed bulb or root? Did you
forage or sleep

in the mornings—oh Dodo, what
did you eat,

were your days not so bitter
but sweet? Did the flies fly

right by you or did
they land,

did you lose your better self
when you rotted in the sand?

I think I've stirred
you from where

you did not wish
to wake—I think I've shaken

all the flowers from your shade.

Maybe I shouldn't
dig you up like a dog, or maybe

I should—see my hands,
what makes them

open, so sure of what
they will find?

I dreamt my stomach was full of stones

they fed to me
at night to do the grinding.

I died eventually.

Death was not darker than the pen
they kept you in.
I thought it mild,
just barely wet

feeling.
I lost my beak in it,
then lost it again.

*

Now they're cleaning me out
with wadded cheesecloth.
I'm ribbed now, I'm raw,
the color of lard.

They plump me with cotton
and stuff me with sawdust
and fluff. My tail

is newly tufted.
They cinch me with hen feathers
in my bald spots.

These days,
I look through marbled glass,
and they cry me tears
with candle wax.

The lead scattered through your cranial bone

glints like fool's gold, like glittering pyrite,
on the micro-CT scan, softly whirring—
which is all that's left of your skull we kept.

Latest discovery: you were shot in the back
of the head. Who knows where or when—
the Oxford professors find it impossible

to guess how your final act played out,
whether you arrived in London
alive or dead. It took us this long to know

we drew you wrong—
un-straightened your back, saddled
your breast with extra weight, forged

your likeness after birds overstuffed,
the few that made it back to Europe
fattened for sake of curiosity:

a penny paid to see and feed.
Now scientists carry you in purple
rubber gloves—delicate, cradling

the skin on half your head intact,
like a monk's hood, like a swimmer's
cap—as a scatter of pellets appears

on the same luminous digital screen
used for murder trials by forensics teams.
The machine whirrs on and on

*

into the wilds of the seventeenth century. All is stillness
and heat—no line between sky and sea, no
ribbon of breeze to make the palm fronds
flinch. I am holding my gun heavy with shot,
I am eyeing you on the beach—

(Once we swept fish from the sea. Once
you were an egg on a grassy bed.)

          And gone so swiftly: gone
tidal winds and forest floors for nesting, gone
trees bearing fruit and island shadows
lengthening. The shot sprayed from my aim,
smooth and muzzle-loaded, fired from my
shoulder, the blow-back smoke, white sulfurous
cloud, puff of feathers into air.

They called you melancholy, too.

They called you blue. In the ship's hold
that would not hold the world,
they shuttled you below.

Didn't you know you were fit for a king?

But you would not eat.
No sugar, no bread, no
feathery crumb.

More than once, they tried to force your beak.

Sometimes I think you see
a version of me—

Farther off, large islands float,

green with unstoppable prairies,
but you had one island and asked
for none more.

Who wouldn't salt the world,
given salt? Who, given seed,
wouldn't sow in flowering rows?

A kick, a coax,
it didn't take much.

When you died, they had to throw
you overboard.

You, again,

all sea-brain
and moon-feet—
your plush wide awake
with cities of fleas.

Did I step out
of your mouth,
or did you
step in? Once, I was given
maps of attachment,

but along the way
I lost them.
Dodo, I'm sorry
to make you
so sorry. In bare

air,
a bullet stilled.
Dawdle-you-do.
Now I'm marsh-faced,
like you,

I'm stiff-collared
and preening.
I woke today
half dodo
and half daughter—

was it you I saw
    waiting,
        under the pale
of the water?
    You,

with your feathers
    thickened with brine,
        your pieced beak,
tar-dipped
    to shine.

So legged, so footed, and who's left to care?

So your days bottomed out, so your luck stuttered then stopped.

So here a foot,
a pinioned wing,

                            so ankle, thigh, and shoulder blade.

So here your weight, the heft you heaved, so tiny feathers
cleaned out by spring.

Now absolute, now by-gone blur—

you're bottom in a bottomland,
dead dodo in a drawer.

So here your head, your out-sized brain,
your stomach they called greasy,

                                 your throat that rang.

So legged and footed, so loosened
from one world—

you used to sleep undone

beneath the moon: gun-barrel

moon like a mouth

about to open wider.

Notes

"Calenture"

In his article "Scorbutic Nostalgia," Jonathan Lamb describes calenture as an affliction suffered by sailors in which the "victim hallucinates a pastoral landscape on the ocean's back, and does everything possible to enter it." Lamb argues that, "in their effects on the senses and the passions," calenture and scurvy's scorbutic nostalgia "are in effect the same: they are both ecstatic states of nervous excitement arising from a radical disruption of the victim's sense of position in time and space." The line "Those affected had a fierce look" is drawn from Ephraim Chambers's 1786 *Cyclopaedia*, which Lamb also quotes: "Those affected have a fierce look, and are very unruly, being so eager to get to their imaginary cool verdure."

"Sometimes My Body Lifts as a Wave"

In the mid-to-late 1850s, William Walker, an American "filibuster" obsessed with conquest and widening American imperialism, invaded Nicaragua, named himself President, and incited war; when his tenuous power collapsed, Walker fled Granada and ordered his general George F. Henningsen to raze and burn the city. Apocryphal or not, a restaurant in Granada is said to have a wall marked with bullet holes from an attempted execution of Walker, who was later killed by firing squad in Honduras.

"So I Try to Picture the Priests," "On the New Continent, Our Eyes Shining," and "'I have written myself into a Tropical glow'"

Andrea Wulf's *The Invention of Nature* about Alexander von Humboldt provided a historical lens that sparked these poems into being. Specifically, I am indebted to Wulf's quotation from Charles Darwin's journals, which provided me with a title, and her descriptions of Humboldt's travels in South America.

"Scurvy"
In his book *Scurvy: The Disease of Discovery*, Jonathan Lamb writes, "Although the most common symptom in the later stages was severe debility and lassitude, it was remarkable how often sensory impressions were enlarged in scurvy, as if the neuromodulators had been put out of action, and there were no longer any inhibitions to sensory excitement. Smells became overwhelming, often disgusting yet sometimes exquisite; sights were dazzling; sounds fascinating or intolerable; the sense of touch morbidly acute; and taste fatally voluptuous. Sailors often died from pleasure in the moment they ate the fruit and drank the sweet water for which they had been yearning."

"Steller and the Sea Cow"
After being shipwrecked in 1741 on Bering Island as part of Vitus Bering's expedition, Georg Wilhelm Steller studied the enormous sea cow, a cold-water, herbivore relative of the manatee that could reach thirty feet in length. Steller later described the sea cow, as well as other animals, in his *De bestiis marinis*, or *The Beasts of the Sea*. Some details in the poem are drawn directly from his observations. The sea cow is believed to have gone extinct by the 1760s, less than thirty years after Steller encountered it.

"The Mermaids at Weeki Wachee"
This poem, as all the other poems in the collection, was written on stolen land. I'm indebted to Jennifer A. Kokai's article, "Weeki Wachee Girls and Buccanner Boys: The Evolution of Mermaids, Gender, and 'Man versus Nature' Tourism," for invaluable context and research that inspired it. Also indispensable: Lu Vickers's *Weeki Wachee: City of Mermaids*, the video "Sirens of the Deep Mermaid Camp at Weeki Wachee Springs" viewed on YouTube, and the 2007 documentary *Endangered Mermaids: The Manatees of Florida*.

"Sometimes I Am Permitted to Return to the Sea"
The title is adapted from Robert Duncan's poem "Often I Am
Permitted to Return to a Meadow."

"So Legged and Footed"
The dodo lived solely on what is now the island-nation of Mauritius
in the Indian Ocean. A large-bodied bird with small, flightless wings,
the dodo had no natural predators. Less than a hundred years after
humans arrived on the island (bringing with them invasive species
such as rats and pigs), the dodo was extinct.

The sequence takes its title from Sir Hamon L'Estrange's description
of a dodo held in captivity in London: "About 1638, as I walked
London streets, I saw the picture of a strange looking fowle hung out
upon a clothe and myselfe with one or two more in company went in
to see it. It was kept in a chamber, and was a great fowle somewhat
bigger than the largest Turkey cock, and so legged and footed, but
stouter and thicker and of more erect shape, coloured before like the
breast of a young cock fesan, and on the back of a dunn or dearc
colour. The keeper called it a Dodo, and in the ende of a chymney in
the chamber there lay a heape of large pebble stones, whereof hee
gave it many in our sight, some as big as nutmegs, and the keeper
told us that she eats them (conducing to digestion), and though I
remember not how far the keeper was questioned therein, yet I am
confident that afterwards she cast them all again."

In the 1860s, British schoolteacher George Clark traveled to
Mauritius in hopes of finding, and bringing back to Europe, dodo
bones. In his *Account of the late Discovery of Dodos' Remains in the
Island of Mauritius*, Clark writes: "[A]fter many fruitless visits to the
spot [in the Mare aux Songes swamp], and inspection of the bones
turned up as the work went on, I resolved on sending some men into

the centre of the marsh, where the water was about three feet deep; and there, by feeling in the mud with their naked feet, they met with one entire tibia, a portion of another, and a tarso-metatarsus. I informed [landowner] Mr. de Bissy of my success, at which he was greatly delighted; and he kindly gave me the exclusive right to every bone that might be found there, refusing to some applicants permission to search there, saying that, as the discovery was entirely mine, he considered that I had a prescriptive right to all the bones."

Much is unknown about the Oxford Dodo, also called the Tradescant Dodo after the Tradescant Ark collection from which it came. Now housed in the Oxford University Museum of Natural History, it consists of a head and foot, including skin, bone, and traces of feathers, and was long believed to be the remains of the same bird L'Estrange observed in London in 1638. However, in 2018, scientists using CT scanning discovered that the Oxford Dodo had been shot in the back of the head with lead pellets, like those of fowling shot, giving rise to as yet unanswered questions about the bird's origin and death.

photo by Juan Meneses

Allison Hutchcraft grew up in California and received her MFA from Purdue University. Her poems have appeared in *Boulevard, The Cincinnati Review, The Gettysburg Review, Kenyon Review, The Missouri Review,* and *The Southern Review,* among other journals. A former resident at the Sitka Center for Art and Ecology on the Oregon coast, she has been awarded a fellowship from the North Carolina Arts Council and scholarships from the Key West Literary Seminars, the Tin House Writers Workshop, and the Community of Writers. She teaches creative writing at the University of North Carolina at Charlotte.

The New Issues Editor's Choice